Keep the Singing

poems by

Liza Porter

Finishing Line Press
Georgetown, Kentucky

Keep the Singing

Copyright © 2021 by Liza Porter
ISBN 978-1-64662-641-0 First Edition
All rights reserved under International and Pan-American Copyright Conventions. No part of this book may be reproduced in any manner whatsoever without written permission from the publisher, except in the case of brief quotations embodied in critical articles and reviews.

ACKNOWLEDGMENTS

Adagio for Strings, *Diner*, Fall/Winter 2005
All these things," 2007, *The Chrysalis Reader*, " [in Imagine That! Breaking Through to Other Worlds, a Chrysalis Reader]
A Sort of Sigh," *The Blind Man's Rainbow*, Spring 2005, Volume X, Issue 3
Blue Gloves, Stars, *Cobalt Review*, Winter 2014, http://www.cobaltreview.com.
Body Count, *Gingko Tree Review*, Volume 3, Number 1, 2006
Say we had poetry then, 2006; All these things, 2010; Northern California Where You Still Live, 2012, *Blue Mountain Arts*, http://www.sps.com/poetry/
The Major, *The MacGuffin*, Fall 2012.
Trains, *Pebble Lake Review*, 2005
Trains and The Major also appeared in *Red Stain* (2014, Finishing Line Press)

Publisher: Leah Huete de Maines
Editor: Christen Kincaid
Cover Art: Ariel G. Porter
Author Photo: Andrea Conway
Cover Design: Elizabeth Maines McCleavy

Order online: www.finishinglinepress.com
also available on amazon.com

Author inquiries and mail orders:
Finishing Line Press
PO Box 1626
Georgetown, Kentucky 40324
USA

Table of Contents

Sister 1

The Vigil 2

Sing a song for her leaving 3

All these things 4

The Major 5

Going Home 6

Say we had poetry then 7

Northern California, Where You Still Live 9

Trains 11

Edie, if you hear Dylan singing 13

A Sort of Sigh 14

She and I sit on the floor 15

Blue Gloves, Stars 16

Elegy for Edie 17

Adagio for Strings 18

The Therapist 20

Your heart remains intact 21

Cremation 22

The time you have 23

The Music 24

Elegy in Blue 25

Keep the singing 26

Poem for Edie on Thanksgiving 27

American Graffiti 28

Or by wings 29

The Light 30

*For Edith Marie Lavis,
1953-2005 R.I.P.*

Sister

Sometimes when I think of O'Keeffe
I see
rusty orange petals
and myself
at twelve
going to you in the night
when the blood came.

The Vigil

We talk to her and read
and pray and sing
as candles flame all around her
and one woman even dances
as I lie down next to the table
in the small living room
where my sister waits for us
to say enough good-byes
to let her pass to the other world.
As the days march, first, second, third
my sister's eyes sink deeper into her face
as if retreating from this fiery place
to another, calmer existence.
Yes, she looks calm. Isn't that the only thing
the living can know—the dead
seem peaceful and calm, or maybe
they are finally done with the pain?

The flowers in my sister's hands
as she lies on the table
after the women wash her body
before the men lift her into the casket
on the fourth morning after her death,
are gone now. The flowers are gone,
her hands are gone. And her fingers
and the dark blue polish on her nails
the turquoise knit hat,
the scarf someone wrapped around her neck
to keep her warm,
the hat, the scarf, the poem I wrote
and placed in the casket,
the note from her daughter,
certain pages torn out of books,
Kinnell, Rich, Philip Levine
drawings of eagles and flaming yellow circles
that look like rising suns.

Sing a song for her leaving, her soul
rising years ago into tarnished skies
below this same half-moon, her blue eyes closed
to this world, restless spirit open
to the next. Crows cry overhead, mist rises
from the canyon, the smoke of funeral pyres,
the Pacific Ocean and its ancient fires
hide this cold pen, these frigid fingers
mining these words for some glimpse of new wings
the eye of Venus on the horizon
watching the earth turn without her,
and spring calls forth its new grass
and persimmon blossoms, bright orange
as the sun when it sets, places them
on the ground at the sky's feet.

All these things

I found our grandmother's long black coat
in the hallway closet next to where you fell

that morning. I'm wearing the knit hat
your husband gave you when your hair

started going, ice blue cashmere, the color
at the edge of a desert sky in winter,

there are matching gloves, too, sister
the old-fashioned kind that go halfway up the arms,

but you know all this, the gloves are inside on the table,
the scarf lost, he gave me all these things of yours to take home

three pairs of shoes, piano music, a file folder
full of your poems, but you know this, you were with us

hovering in the rooms of your house pointing out
all these things we'd never noticed, while we stumbled

around on the polished wood floors like the deaf and blind
in our clumsy clinging grief, one friend says she cried

for half an hour when she came inside the day of the service,
your purse open on the desk as if you'd be back to grab it

any minute, now she imagines only peace, she says
your shiny new wings, a better place she can only guess at

while those of us with the same blood in our veins
and all these things still wander in a spiral of why, how, what

could have been and will keep wandering until
all these things have been folded into stacks, hidden

in drawers and closets, given away, sorted out, divided up
and laid to rest.

The Major

What you have heard is true. I went to his house.
His children sit at the dinner table like soldiers.
There are newspapers, cloth napkins, cases of
bourbon in a closet with his Marine Corps dress blues.
The sun is a bruised cheek falling into the ocean.
The windows of the house are locked. Unspoken words
hang on the chain-link fence in the back yard like
escaping convicts. Walter Cronkite recites body counts
from the living room. He names no names. We eat
roast beef, potatoes, carrots. All the children are asked
what they'd learned in school that day. When the youngest
doesn't answer, the Major takes a sip of his whiskey and
goes on to the next one. "Nothing," he says, his face a war
mask. The rest of them inhale in unison. The older girl says to
the younger with her elbow: Say nothing. The older boy
says in a soft voice, eyes down: "I learned something in Latin
class." The dog licks my hand under the table. No one
looks up from their food. The butter melts in its crystal dish.
The grandmother says "More biscuits?" and offers the plate
to the mother, who shakes her head and stands up.
"Dessert?" she asks. The children look at her like puppies ready
for a leash and an open door. The Major says: "They eat too much
as it is," and drinks more whiskey. The grandmother stands
and starts to clear the dishes. The boy who had learned nothing
stands, too. The chair legs scrape the floor. The Major gulps
the rest of his drink, knuckles white around the glass. "Sit down,"
he says. The boy who had learned nothing ignores him
and keeps walking. The sisters hold hands under the table.
The dog's tail tickles my bare leg. The dog growls.

The form and tone of this poem were borrowed from
"The Colonel" by Carolyn Forche

Going Home

When I go back thirty years later and the old man
asks me in, the light almost blinds me, this God-white presence—
his wife, resting, a week past breast surgery
her beatific smile, the recliner placed where
a dividing wall used to be. They got it all, the old man beams
and shows me outside, the back yard a jungle, the exact one
I'd dreamed of, wildflowers and blooming citrus and smooth green
grass. I remember my grandmother's sweet peas along the back fence,
lavender and pink and white, and the ghost-yellow lawn that never
quite thrived, you could have flamed the whole fucking thing with a
single smoking match. I don't mention to the old guy that
my sister died three days before of the very same disease.

Say we had poetry then
something to pull our drowning bodies
out of the sea of fear we struggled in every day.
Say we sat in the dark of our room, backs against your twin bed,
feet pointed toward mine, toenails shining
under the moon as it peeked through a crack
in the drapes, a small flashlight illuminating the pages
of some book that appeared from the sky—*Out of nowhere*
we would say. *Maybe God sent it.*

Say we had poetry then and the words in that book
pierced our hearts as cupid would much later in our lives,
opened them wide with awe and hope, like the hymns
we'd sing in church choir dressed in pale blue robes
performing in a different way than we had to
the rest of the week at home. Say this book of poems
fell from the sky into our laps one night, the words
filling our souls with so much light
we couldn't hold it, we would burst into stars.
We had to make up our own songs—me the melody, you the harmony,
and those songs were ours, forever, we would never forget them.

Say we had poetry then and our songs drifted out the open window
and floated into that southern California night, the sky
balmy with the ocean so close by, what if our voices
swam into the mist that gathered in droplets on car windows
by morning and burned off by noon, like the blue fog did
each Sunday on the coast in summer, by the time we got to our haven,
the beach, and ran from the station wagon across the sand
into the waves without a sound
and floated out into the water
as if we'd found a new womb to rock us.

Say we had poetry then, and our songs flew out the window
of our room and into the neighbors' houses the next morning
through screen doors, the sound so sweet—who can possibly resist
the voices of innocent girls—and what if those songs
somehow transformed their lives, as they couldn't ours,
for our paths were preordained, I see now,
but what if the words that escaped from our throats back when
darkness was safer than light, when silence seemed the only
reasonable reply, say those songs actually
made it out from between our lips
and helped someone live a better life. Made the Vietnam war death
of Lieutenant Jordan next door easier for his widow and daughters
to bear, made the eyes of those two ugly girls in the house
on the other side shine with themselves and their fate.
Say we had poetry then, later, of course, after the light
became safe, after the silence became unbearable.

Northern California, Where You Still Live

Alone in the dark on the wooden deck
facing west, it's silent except for a few cars
flying by on a road in the distance.

The Jeffers' book to my left holds your
favorite poems of the Pacific, granite
rock, salt, the day moon. Yesterday

Mark and I drove to the coast, spoke
of old times, dark and light, cried
when tears were due. You are not gone

but still live in the sea that speaks
its gray morning tides, its secret sorrows, its
whispers of fine mist and light.

We cannot touch you in the way we've
always taken for granted, but our fingers will
spread and reach to the hills between here

and there where you still sing in your
true voice, your a cappella song
needs no accompaniment. You are

ocean now. The waves of yesterday
rock my feet as we walk and gaze
at shimmering water and see

Point Reyes off in the distance,
that dark peninsula showing itself
only a few times in winter and only

under clear skies. Soon your ashes will fly
above a warmer ocean, and we
will hear your voice in the tide that

flows out and in from the shore
and back out to sea, over and
over and over, forever.

Trains
     for E.D.

This early in the morning the clouds have cleared
and I can hear the whistle of train after train
rolling across the desert five miles south in the dark.

I remember trains, the one that carried you north
to the forest in autumn when no other mode of travel
was good enough. But we had our own, didn't we,

the warm tongue of dope, cool teeth of booze
the dirty fingers of men whose names we
never remembered no matter how hard we tried.

What was it about us we hated so much?
Sleeping in strangers' beds was easier than even
approaching that age-old question. The ratty motor lodge

just south of Newport that summer, its depression-ware
dishes in dull primary colors, the muddy spring
trickling down to the beach like blood from a cut.

No one could ever sweep all the grit off those
chipped linoleum tiles. The two brothers who owned the place,
what did the older one's hands feel like on your skin?

I met a man just after you left, when we pushed back
from the bar and headed out to his house
he was the nicest guy I'd ever known in my life.

But there were Nam-ghosts in those walls, shadows
of his petrified wife and kids, he had to shower
just after we did it on the living room floor.

He spread out a blanket first and quoted Genesis to me.
The tracks were just behind his back fence and I saw myself
running beside those shrieking metal rails

nothing but the clothes on my back and a photo
of you in my pocket, your scared eyes staring
at nothing. I jumped up into an empty car

heading east or west, it didn't make any difference.
When I caught my breath, I glanced back toward town.
Not a single soul was watching.

Edie, if you hear Dylan singing

It's all right ma, I'm only crying
remember:
Mesa Ampitheater the summer Ariel
was born, my breasts leaking
milk, a scarf tied round your head
white silk trailing behind you, and then:
his harmonica wailing
into the hot steamy sky.

A Sort of Sigh

Someone came into my room last night
and spoke the truth. A voice quiet
as God, but I knew it. A ripple
of water in the womb, the hum
of blood, someone outside,
playing old love songs. I thought
it was you on the front porch
singing stories of places you've been,
friends whose souls you
memorized as if your favorite music.
Now I see only the blue door to your
right, its gold knob, the brick wall
opposite. You sit. Your eyes flit
back and forth, squinting, trying
to decide which one to
choose. A tapping comes from behind
the door, then the wall, the door,
the wall, drumbeats in a rhythm
I can't detect. Synco-
pation, you say. It's all uneven
counts, ta *da*, ta *da*, ta *da*. There are
no rests until the very end.
I close my eyes to listen. When I open
them, you're gone, your body
a faint impression on the wall, arms wide,
legs bent as if running. A sort of sigh
escapes the bricks. A sort of
waving good-bye.

She and I sit on the floor
in my living room going through boxes of photographs, trying to remember when they were taken, and writing the years on the back of each one. She pulls out a picture from 15 years before—me posing in front of the fireplace in the duplex where I lived with my toddler daughter—all dressed up in a purple dress with big white flowers, a big smile on my face, for a job interview at a law firm. She holds up the picture, sort of shakes it to make sure I see it, and says "What's so wrong with that?" I immediately know what she means. Why did we think we were so ugly, so despicable? Why did we hate ourselves so much?

Blue Gloves, Stars

Forgive me, I have almost forgotten your face
in the years you've been gone, I have ruined
your blue cashmere gloves, there is pencil lead smudged
on the fingers of the right one from writing
outside in winter, a gaping hole
on the tip of the middle finger, a snag on the knuckle of the thumb
where the yarn is unraveling like time, forgive me
I spilled coffee on one of your stories—the long one about green glass
and stars, a woman abandoned in the dark
I have changed the glass and stars to the pale sea blue
of your gloves, but most of all forgive me
for pretending the story is mine, I know that is cheating
you, me, the dead, the living, but think of the universe
its fickle lights and lies—I want something
of you to be me, I want you to be a story, or a film I can watch every day
I'll keep watching and watching until the stars say
their last lines and fall dead on the floor, the celluloid flops
on its reel after the credits roll, the sound of a train going by but not
the ending of the movie will comfort me, as if seeing
death on the screen can cancel dying itself or at least conceal you
as you fly across a sweeping panorama of the Pacific Ocean
where we floated singing as children and built sand castles as high
as our unlived lives, I forgive you for being the first to die—
before her time people say when someone leaps
and rises above the earth to reach the other world
before we think they should, forgive me
if I am not convinced this is true.

Elegy for Edie

I keep wondering about the pain
before she took her last breath
and what she saw—
I can't stop—they say she fell, broken
to the floor, arms flailing
as if a thunder storm came and went in just a few seconds,
they say it was over almost before it began. I know pain—
not exactly the killing kind, but that snake through
the belly over too many years of not being able to want, or even ask
for anything, or sisters living with smiling masks on their faces.
Some call it life's lessons, some sort of plan—no pain, no gain
they say around the tables, those who know
exactly what they're talking about, those
with stories some can't even manage to dream—
their nights full of pale pink ballerinas and silk sheets—well,
we didn't quite end up on the street like some of the others
but who can give the exact name to the paths
others walk on?—asphalt or dirt or those tiny bits of gravel
that burrow into bare feet if your shoes are
lost. I sat with her many times while we
dug those sharp stones out of our skin, eyeing
each other, saying—this isn't so bad,
look how slow the bleeding.

Adagio for Strings

As we do this
music, this thing.
That whisper, this bruise
Barber's strings.

So separate, but joined
we sing.
And slip like liquid
down the strings.

As we do this
pleasure to
each other so
close to the pain.

As we do this
music, cells sing.
This pleasure so
close to the sting.

Reach higher each time
we scream. Every
time we
do, we change.

As we do this
pleasure to
each other so
close to the pain.

As we do this
music, I weep.
No time
no space, the strings

so high, then
quiet again, so
soon past screaming
the pain.

As we do this
pleasure
to each other
close to the pain.

The Therapist

When I visit him a month after she dies, he says
the last time he saw her she practically danced into his office,
beaming—
an ethereal light around her, he says—
and she grinned at him and she said "I'm done with this,"
meaning the incest work they'd done together, he thinks. After her
uterus is taken, before the small mass on her brain stem and the
radiation snatches her away. "I'm done with this," he tells me she said,
and I avoid his eyes, my stomach lurching, and I think:
She quit. She gave up the battle we've fought
our whole lives, together sometimes, to retrieve what was
stolen from us—our innocence, our bodies, even each other.

Yesterday, making love with my husband, sudden clouds
rubbing the sky with charcoal shadows outside our naked
windows, I stop breathing between movement
and rest, and weep one more time for the past,
hear her again: "I'm done with this." And I see his office and
the golden light, her shining face, as if I'm there
and I know, then, that I *am* there, and what
she means to say is: "I've finished what I came here to do."

Your heart remains intact

> *look / where / Christ's / blood*
> *streams*
> *in / the / fir- / ma / ment*
> *look / where / your*
> *broth- / er*
> *is*
> *splash / 'd*
> *a- / gainst*
> *the*
> *sky*
>   "Untitled" by Robert Lax

If you were a bird, you'd be a night dove in the presence of close stars, your soul
stretched taut, your wings drawing zeroes in the black sky.

We align your body on an axis, east to west at the base of Paradise, green fish easing
toward imagined green, perfumed river sings, the moon burns red in circling fires.

We make lists: incense; ashes; relations; look up, look elsewhere, as if something might
save you; do not dare to utter the word Peace.

Our bodies kneeling, blindfolded, dawn rises, trembling, the moon abandons the sky
with nothing to show but its closed eye, our hearts trained, your bronze blood, for whom

do the stars yearn? The sea that was promised? You, with eyes fixed on a distant
watchtower? Wind crawls up the road, ready to spring into disappeared stars.

Shutters knock in stuttering voices to mimic our grief. The ocotillos moan their desire
for everything. Nothing.

Cremation

There is no grave for her, no specific place I can kneel down with
roses or daisies or wild sage, no cemetery plot on which to
place them, no bones and flesh in the ground dissolving to nothing,
she is already nothing, the unvarnished pine box with vines and
flowers carved around the top edge and
ropes on four corners for lifting, gone
to the place where her body—her eyes, her nerves, her blood—
were burned—the fire, I can see the fire, I can hear its
roaring, its orange and blue and white-hot flames reach up
as if to secure her spot in the heavens, how can I speak
or sing to her if there is no place where she is, no
granite headstone etched with her name and the years she
lived, how can I possibly know she's gone if
I can't touch something, grass or stone or her name, if I can't watch
daylight shine on the flowers I put there on a visit
to her last home, no, it's not really a last home they say she
still lives in our hearts they say she's in the Light they say
in the Light they say in the Light. Fuck the Light.

The time you have

Your path is the same as our mothers and theirs before them,
giving birth to beings who will shoot away like arrows to the stars
neither of us can name. Above a world made not of the peace

we hoped for, but noisy carnival rides and houses of horror.
Funhouse mirrors reflect the guilt in our eyes at what
we have left them. But there is still cello music, viola,

the piano, your fingers move so quickly on the keys
as you try to sustain your daughters' naked convictions.
And there's the kitchen counter, raw food changed into the art

you wish you made and don't realize you'd already started.
The sewing of clothes for your family may seem nothing
like a published poem, it's the constant hum of the machine

that keeps you going, the pale light shining on the needle
that reveals your longing. Fabric, paper, lines of colored thread
so like pen on vellum, you can't deny it any more. To withstand

our world's dive into darkness, you instill in them the red passion
that streams through your veins with or without your intention.
You watch them skate onto thin ice, your heart no longer

the territory they inhabit. They'll manage the loops
and twirls absorbed from others' teachings, while the art
you crave to make spins around you, a spirit dancing

a dervish. She holds out her hands. She is right before you,
an apparition, a thing changing form. All the recipes
you memorize, all the curtains you stitch

with which to hide from the dark are the same as any poem
you might have written, any painting you could create.

The Music

To write a song for the small pile of wood on the south
side of my sister's house
in northern California—one long piece of tree trunk, several gnarled
branches and a stubby cracked stump.

But what about the kindling-sized pieces almost hidden under
the others? Are they too small
to be bothered with? Or a slight success—say, the playing of a perfect
measure played by
a child on the cello—so insignificant unless we listen with more than
our ears. Why is

the fog that drifts in from the ocean seen by some as a nuisance
instead of the mystery
it really is? I want to start noticing small things. The cello. The way
my sister and her
husband sing a cappella in harmony in my niece's bedroom at night
and the music flows

straight down the hall through the hollow sliding doors into the room
where I'm reading
as if in a dream.

Elegy in Blue

> *To go in to get to—or to go through*
> *to get beyond.*   Jami Macarty

When a sister leaves, at the winter solstice something goes,
the sun or moon, a certain slant of blue, a shadow or a certain

twist of soul, a gold shine remaining behind, spiraling.
When a sister goes, though leaving has its seasons, time stops

on that ground, feet leave prints in desert or sea or mind, waves
of wind or water; a swirl of soul, something survives to haunt

or advise or give more than the body which holds it. When
a sister leaves, the body is not the heart, though the heart-blood

keeps the body—and the heart-body does not prove appearance
or spirit or hope the way blue light plays on a cold sea, or sand

allows each grain its perfection to exist. When a sister goes
she leaves open windows and doors, more of these

than before, and more than that and when she leaves
there is singing in minor keys, and yet the music

flees that minority, its memory ascends into free space, wind,
aquamarine sky, an eye-beacon seeking true north.

When a sister leaves, her voice does not go with her
but sings and whistles, or howls or moans, perhaps

with relief, or release and that is how we believe the going.

Keep the singing

She gave me thunder, the road
she gave me the poets, the poems,
the words still blare from the parchment
like horns, the ancient paper still flutters in the sun, the fog, the rain
she gave me the lips of death, Woolf, Sexton, Plath,
she gave me the headlights, a highway to follow
named 61, its white line still there in the distance
like hope, my heart pulled by a long Pythagorean string down roads
filled with cars and girls and slamming screens, she pulled
the sadness from my ears and made me hear, she gave me
death and needles, neck shivers, she gave me poems
as if they were her very own, she said borrow, don't steal, she gave me
alphabets, chords, the minor keys, she gave me rock-
n-roll, she gave me the great song traveler, he still
screams from the vinyl and the tapes, she gave me something
to wait for, she gave me fate, her taste
for the way an image can slap you in the face, she gave me
longing, she gave me waiting, the desire to
keep the waiting, keep the waiting, she said, not from
my lips but from theirs, the others, the thunder, the road
the idiot wind, from the ones who sing with hidden tongues,
she gave me want and need and the ability to see,
to believe, she said don't fake it, wait for the real thing
don't fake it, don't give in she said keep the singing
she said keep the singing keep the singing.

Poem for Edie on Thanksgiving

After two years, as we gather family and food
as easily as in the past, and the desert

waits for winter to speak, beyond the glass
everything has changed, and nothing.

You are north, or south, anywhere, not here,
in a bright room with new poems

at your feet, there are candles flaming white
and maybe the hearts of children who did not survive

this world. Even you had to walk away, blue
flowers in your hands, as if an offering to your new

home, held high like stalks of sage to clear the space
you would go. But we see none of this, and in the end

little matters but the immense wheel of yearning,
our eyes never quite wet enough, grief's weight still heavy

if only for mourning's sake. I am sorry
to keep you like this, burying you, lifting you up

again and again, I think it may hold you back, the exact
opposite of wind blowing, scattering its seeds, or poems,

and no one can hear this except you, but you have
already changed to air. I hang worn fabric

from the back patio beam to block the wind, it is
sometimes too much to bear. I wish I could smudge you

into something else, let you go, as smoke
from a fireplace floats into the sky—

a visible thing, instead of this eternal questioning.

American Graffiti
laughing hysterically
one of us quoting a teenage hot-rod movie we saw
four or five times back in the day, where the college-bound boy—
after the teen gangsters hold him hostage and
pocket all the pinball machine change—
stutters to the owner of the diner: *He means
we're all done having loads of fun out here,*
the alpha thug's eyes tracking his every move.

Or by wings

I meant to write first of headlights,
your poem beams from blue pages

on the kitchen table before me.
Please help me with this, I cry

to your invisible face, to the sky.
Highways and headlights and trains,

we couldn't stop moving till the desert
opened its prickly arms to claim us.

Remember when we couldn't even cry
you ask from somewhere, not here,

our stoicism shadowed only by the will
to survive? In this desert, sister, my eyes

ache for the true green of Oregon pines, tears dry
before reaching the trembling mouth,

the mountains have nowhere near the height
of those in the north, they begin

on the desert floor and do not rise all the way
to heaven. I hear Dylan sing: sad-eyed lady of the lowlands

as I watch you leave, one last time—
maybe by car, maybe by train, or by wings.

The Light

1.
It was the light that birthed us first, slower than sunrise,
shocking us all into silence. Then the moon,
its dull plodding, reflected our longing till morning.
When the sun appeared, some fell to their knees
and wept, others slept in timid exhaustion.
Through the light, I saw your stardust bed, body still
in the shine before us. You gave us what we thought
we had lost: children growing in the sun, love
of the blinding light, a kind of singing.

2.
We don't know this desert or anything about how
God works or any sort of plan. We think we can track
our path through time. But when the sun moves
through the sky the way a virus invades a body
or a drug tames a vein, we wonder what it's really like up there
in the clouds, that yellow star burning, one among trillions,
not strange at all to someone viewing it like you
from above. And when the moon appears before dark,
we say: we don't need you yet, our eyes are accustomed
to squinting, we wait for the black rain to heal the stinging.
Our tears mean nothing except relief from missing you.
You have no halo, no special light, but the memory of a face
as bright as that moon when darkness falls.

3.
I have light too, but not the whole thing. Of course I think:
was there something else I could have done? Do I have a
monopoly on going forward, or even round and round in my
tortured orbit? Is your light one of those stars by now?
I will some day glance sideways in the deep black and see
the brilliance of your flame. I know it will never

burn out. You are no more mine than the sky.
I will always track the light.

Liza Porter's poem "The day my brother meets Bob Dylan …" appeared in *Visiting Bob: Poems Inspired by the Life and Work of Bob Dylan*, in 2018. Her poetry chapbook *Red Stain* was published by Finishing Line Press in 2014 and was finalist for both the 2015 Arizona New Mexico Book Award and the 2015 WILLA Award (Women Writing the West). Porter received the 2009 Mary Ann Campau Memorial Poetry Fellowship from the University of Arizona Poetry Center. She is founding director of the Other Voices Women's Reading Series at Antigone Books in Tucson, Arizona. Porter's manuscript "Bruce Springsteen Sang to Me" was finalist for the 2019 Cleveland State University Essay Collection Competition, the 2018 Faulkner Society Faulkner-Wisdom Narrative Nonfiction Book Award, the 2018 Tucson Festival of Books Master's Workshop Competition, and the Santa Fe Writers Workshop nonfiction book award. Her essays and poetry have been published in numerous magazines and anthologies, including *The Write Launch, PRISM International, Chautauqua, Cobalt Review, Passages North, The Progressive, AGNI, Diner, Cimarron Review, Barrow Street, Pedestal Magazine, and in What Wildness is this: Women Write About the Southwest* (University of Texas Press: Austin, 2007), and *Poets on Prozac: Mental Illness, Treatment and the Creative Process* (The Johns Hopkins University Press, 2008). Three of Porter's essays have been listed as Notable Essays in *Best American Essays*. www.lizaporter.com.

www.ingramcontent.com/pod-product-compliance
Lightning Source LLC
LaVergne TN
LVHW041601070426
835507LV00011B/1246